THE
NEW FRONTIER
multidimensionality

CEDAR RIVERS

BALBOA.
PRESS

A DIVISION OF HAY HOUSE

Balboa Press books may be ordered through booksellers or by contacting:

Balboa Press
A Division of Hay House
1663 Liberty Drive
Bloomington, IN 47403
www.balboapress.com.au
1-(877) 407-4847

ISBN: 978-1-4525-0651-7 (sc)
ISBN: 978-1-4525-0652-4 (e)

Printed in the United States of America

Balboa Press rev. date: 08/08/2012

For Sal who has supported me throughout the journey, and Kins who has been lovingly overseeing this project from the Spirit Worlds. It's been wonderful exploring the mysteries of the hidden realms in such loving and simpatico company.

Contents

REVIEWS

Cedar Rivers has broken new ground in her book The New Frontier *about the seen and unseen paranormal. It takes a lot of courage to write about one's own experiences in this area that few talk about, much less write about them with such conviction. I very much enjoyed this acknowledgement of the other world we live in. It is written beautifully and is supported with her extraordinary photographs of what she has seen and felt.*

—Helen Gill, writer, psychic counsellor

The New Frontier: multidimensionality *will become your new best friend. As you wander and wonder through the beautiful pages of insight, wisdom, and inspiration, something that may have been dormant inside you may awaken. Cedar Rivers is a pioneer and way shower in the personal development, spirituality, and alternative frontiers in Australia. Her lifestyle embodies consciousness that she shares in all she does and with all those whose paths she crosses. This book will potentially change the views of many about our unseen friends. Its cutting edge—new frontier—content is explained in language available to all. I love it.*

—Chris Hooper, Chris Hooper Promotions

Cedar is one of those rare people who one instantly knows can be trusted implicitly. Her book is a joy to read, full of revelations, and will encourage us all to trust our own knowing whilst reconnecting with the world of spirit, which is, all around us, every moment of every day.

—Tamayra Hayman, spiritual intuitive and guide

It is such a pleasure to read your completed book and see your amazing photos of a journey, which has taken many years and which I was honoured to be a part of. Having been there at the Australia Day parade in 2007 where the first magical orbs showed themselves through your camera lens, your journey through this new frontier has expanded into one of unexpected surprises and delights. We need only open our eyes and hearts to see the beauty and true magic of the unseen worlds that surround us. Thank you so much, Cedar, for your creativity, perseverance, and loving acknowledgement of all that is.

—Nina Angelo, OAM, marriage celebrant, artist, and storyteller

The New Frontier is lavishly illustrated with marvellous and spectacular images and offers clear guidance on how to photograph and communicate with spirit orbs and other light beings. It is enriched with wonder and magic, shedding light on what an extraordinary and valuable gift it is to be able to consciously experience multidimensionality. This fascinating journey inspired me to see the world from different perspectives, expanding my awareness of an awe-inspiring universe of new possibilities.

—Sally Brocklehurst, healer, inspirational writer, and speaker

Welcome to the
Unseen Realms

The unseen realms are teeming with souls living their lives in the finer vibrational worlds of spirit. It is exciting to interact with souls such as angels, devas, spirit orbs, nature spirits, and the departed as well as incoming souls. Such contact is no longer only the domain of clairvoyants, clairsentients, and some mystics, as it has been in the past. As the veils between dimensions continue to thin, more can see into the spirit worlds with their physical eyes, as well as with the spiritual third eye.

The miraculous technology of the digital camera has provided the perfect means by which anyone can access the unseen worlds with ease. Throughout the last three decades in particular an ever-growing cornucopia of spiritual subjects has flooded workshops, books, movies, and radio and television programs and swarmed the globe thanks to the far-reaching wonders of the Internet.

Welcome to the Worlds of Spirit

*'Looking through the camera with hearts and minds curious and open,
we may see another side of the magic and mystery that surrounds us.'*
– Sally Brocklehurst

Added to these breakthroughs in awareness of the unseens a
burgeoning awakening to a new spirituality is clearly leading to a
more evolved humanity. More are indeed becoming aware of the
multidimensionality of life and, as a consequence, are experiencing
universal truths and cosmic laws that are credible for all, rather than

dogmas and religious creeds that often fail to give real meaning to a questing person.

Many are now honing their psychic and telepathic abilities, enabling them to readily access the wisdom of their higher selves and the totality of the universal mind. A growing kindness has emerged as more learn the skills of relating through their hearts, which is the way to approach all spirit photography. By developing our paranormal skills, we can have more meaningful contact with spirits as they tirelessly work to create and maintain life in the natural world. We can learn to understand their refined physicality, the functioning of their civilisations, and how they operate in the complex scheme of life.

I bought my first digital camera in early 2007, and a delightful and unexpected bonus has been that I have photographed a wide variety of fascinating phenomena and thousands of the elementals that share our space with us. I've chosen a selection of these photographs to share, accompanied by my current understanding of other realms. I also know that my views may change as I continue to learn more. Thus, this book is a simple primer or introduction to some of the life forms and activity in the invisible worlds, in the hope that it may inspire you to discover more about the multidimensional realms we live in.

I would also like to encourage those of you already photographing the unseens to delve even deeper and consider ways of interacting and helping the spirits in their work for Mother Earth. It can be very rewarding to persevere while studying these photos, as they require a whole new way of seeing. I have often spent hours in front of just one photo on my screensaver or printout, deepening my perspectives by contemplating the shapes as they took form and trusting the intuitive messages that arose. This book is, indeed, one small way I was encouraged by spirit to assist in making these worlds more available.

I have frequently found many beings occupying the same ephemeral substance, and you can see this too when you develop the eye for it. I'm still training myself to see what is less obvious and learning to decipher recognisable forms and messages in clouds, tiles, songs, number plates, and repeating numbers; to look into spaces in nature; to develop an awareness of the activity of birds and animals; and to delve into the meanings of the ever-increasing synchronicities in my daily life.

Another of my joys is sharing these photos with friends, as they invariably see spirits that I haven't noticed. As with all things, we see through our own filters, according to our personal perspectives and experiences. Things that are obvious to me may not be so obvious to others and vice versa. With patience and practice, anyone can learn this alternate way of seeing.

Part one of *The New Frontier* showcases a selection of my photographs of the elementals of earth, air, fire, water, and ether. I've included more examples in the earth and ether sections because those of the fire elementals are all very similar, and many of my air and water elementals take the form of orbs, which I now understand are vehicles for souls, including the human soul. I have also shared some tips on how to photograph spirits at the end of this section.

Part two has an assorted collection of other phenomena that I have found utterly fascinating. The conclusions I've come to are only my initial forays in understanding and, as such, are not definitive, as my discoveries are constantly changing and expanding. I urge you to find your own way in these remarkable adventures, pose lots of questions, be humble, be grateful, persevere, and have fun with the journey. Goddess knows where it will lead.

Where the forest meets the lagoon, beach, ocean, and sky. Can you imagine how many Nature Spirits and other Spirit Beings dwell in these environments? Perhaps there are trillions.

Born a Boomer

My life began just after one of the darkest and most inhumane periods in the history of planet Earth: World War II, which ended in the Western world in 1945. The homecoming of men and women who had been away and the reuniting of couples resulted in a huge upsurge of births of what became known as the "baby boomers." This influx included sensitive souls and "otherworldly" babies born into ordinary families throughout six of the seven continents during the baby boom era. These new souls born from 1946 to 1964 brought with them great changes in consciousness, and later as they matured, they introduced new traditions and innovations.

Activism for equality in the women's and civil rights movements strengthened throughout the 1950s, and the flower power movement of the mid to late '60s heralded another new influx of higher consciousness. Peaceful protesters against the obscenity of the Vietnam War offered flowers, smiles, and songs, rather than aggression or submission to police officers and military personnel. Many remember Woodstock in 1969 and its hundreds of offshoots around the world. The boomers who organized peaceful marches and musical events were some of the original hippies, later to continue their innovations as respected leaders and creative contributors in many diverse fields.

As a young child, I felt sure I was born entirely into the wrong family, in a conservative, Christian farming community in rural Australia. Everything appeared so foreign to me, and I longed for my real home. As a young child, I would gaze into the night sky, marvelling in wonder at the stars while searching the constellations for a connection of authentic belonging.

Although leadership came naturally, I preferred my solitary company instead, delighting in personal musings and discoveries. I relished speed, climbing, running, and my trusty bike, appropriately named Flash, which I'd ride fast and fearlessly for miles in every direction from home, delighting in the great masterpieces of the natural world. Many of us boomers were wild children, just doing what came naturally to us. Life was much simpler in the '40s and

'50s, and most children were fortunate to enjoy total freedom without limitation.

Growing up on farms, I was enthralled by the magic and mystery that accompanied the birth of every wobbly lamb, foal, calf, piglet, kitten, and puppy and by the tentative emergence of tiny, fluffy chickens, ducklings, and wild birds from their shells.

I had a fascination with heights from as early as I can remember and would climb to the highest branches of my favourite trees or scurry up the apricot tree and onto the roofs of the house and adjoining general store that our family owned. Over and over from the peak of the roof, I would run and jump off the edge, believing I could fly high into the air and up and away, and to my great chagrin and sadness, I would find myself falling back to Earth each time.

On many occasions during my seventh and eighth years, I would struggle to climb the slippery iron ladder up to the top flat surface of the tall cement silo, the kind that graced most Australian country towns in the grain-growing districts of that era. I found looking down upon the treetops, tiny ant people, matchbox cars, and houses enthralling. Perspectives such as these stirred memories from deep within and thrilled me no end. These days, I have given up climbing trees and silos, preferring now to satisfy my love of heights by flying in small aircraft and bush walking along high, rocky cliffs.

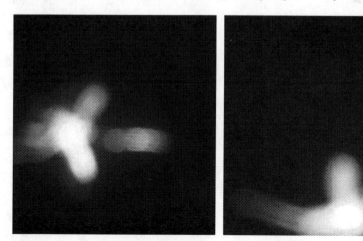

It was during my daily adventures into the gardens and countryside that I first encountered fairies, angels, and other spirits of light. I found little light beings around the huge wild mushrooms that we collected by the bucketful from the paddocks. As a very young child, I saw these ephemeral life forms and communicated with them by thought and chatter, particularly the ones that dwelt in the soft green moss at the base of the huge tree in the back garden. I quickly learned, however, to keep these encounters secret. The people in my life gave more credence to the fairies and elves in fairy-tale books than to the ones I encountered; and the angels preached about in church were deemed real, whereas my angels were the wild imaginings of an unusual child.

Such was my childhood introduction to the unseen spirits of nature, a world with which I continued to engage in privately until, in the '90s, I encountered other people who had similar interests. As a super-sensitive, I have experienced and witnessed many paranormal events throughout my life, including meetings with a remarkable spirit of light in 1967 during a near-death experience, as a result of being in the wrong place when two semitrailers collided with the car in which I was travelling.

In that accident, I sustained severe bleeding and internal injuries and was rushed by ambulance to a nearby hospital where surgeons operated in the very early hours of the morning. I was intrigued to find "myself" watching my body lying on the operating table while "I" observed the fine details of the surgery from an upper corner of the theatre in casualty.

Later, when my mother and sister visited me in intensive care, I related the procedure and conversation between the surgeons throughout the operation to repair me as they removed massive blood clots from my abdomen. Throughout the next few weeks, as I hovered between life and death, I often found "my" consciousness at the ceiling looking down with interest and compassion at my gravely injured body.

On one such occasion, when the pain was unbearably acute, I watched in awe as a glorious tunnel of light manifested before me. The ceiling and walls of the room completely disappeared, and the glowing tunnel felt welcoming and serene. Somehow I knew that place was totally pain free. I understood that, if I chose to enter the tunnel, I would die to the physical and this life, and immediately a tall and magnificent being of pure light appeared. I instantly knew this was a Christed human—one fully in its divinity. Whether this being was a spirit mentor or my own higher self I knew not—neither then nor now. Perhaps they are one and the same.

I marvelled at the translucent luminosity and grace of this being as I prepared to leave my fractured body behind and enter the tunnel. Simultaneously, I felt the words, "You have not yet done what you came to do." And I knew in that moment that I would return my consciousness to the broken body lying on the bed to continue its earthly life.

I was fascinated to find myself re-entering my physical body by "bumping" several times through the wound in my side in the precise millisecond that I made the decision to return. Curiously, all of these unusual events and crystal clear understandings seemed holographic in nature and took "no time" to play out.

I am still learning what I "came to do." Some important aspects have been to garner greater self-knowledge; to create beauty, enjoyment, and harmony; to love; to learn; to hone and refine skills; and to help evolve consciousness, creativity, and kindness. Currently, I endeavour to live life as my optimal self and to share my discoveries with others.

My interest in the worlds of spirit blossomed further in 2007 when I bought a simple digital camera that enabled me to begin photographing the life forms that you see throughout this book, on my Facebook page, and on my websites at www.cedar-rivers.com and www.thenewfrontiermultidimensionality.com.

Humans have extensively explored the earth and outer space. We have travelled to the moon and beyond and all throughout the oceans utilising complex technology, imagination, and intelligence. We have explored physicality, survival, science, religion, and mysticism for eons. Now I believe we have an entirely new frontier to explore—the frontier of the unlimited finer vibrational worlds of multidimensionality and the myriad life forms and cultures that exist in the many dimensions that share our space with us.

If my brief presentations in this little book help you to wonder and if they encourage further enquiry and exploration of the mystery, then I'll be well pleased.

PART ONE

The Elementals

EARTH

EARTH AS MOTHER

More people are discovering what indigenous people, mystics, and
earth-based spiritualists have known for eons—that Mother Earth is
an intelligent, complex, and conscious being and our greatest source
of sustenance, love, and wisdom. Many more are now working in
collaboration with her with respectful and innovative methods of
gardening, farming, manufacturing, eco housing, and land and water
management.

As we learn to access the memories in the archives of the Great Mother, or Gaia as she is known spiritually, we have the opportunity to discover our own sacred connections with her. By doing this, we may come to experience unity with all things in creation.

Mother Earth has, indeed, waited patiently for the masses to connect with her, and more are learning to follow the example of those whose every footstep is mindfully placed where it will do the least damage and whose every action is accompanied by the awareness that she is a conscious, feeling being with a body, heart, and soul.

THE UNSEENS

Knowledge of the worlds of spirit beings is no longer only the domain of sensitives with heightened abilities that are able to attune to the host of dynamic life dwelling within the so-called invisible worlds. Trance dance and drumming, meditation, intention, journeying with hallucinogenic plants, and the remarkable inventions of the digital camera and video recorder have provided others with effective means of connecting with ephemeral life forms, such as nature spirits and angels.

Social networking sites, websites, Internet forums, and a burgeoning number of books on the subject reveal that diligent photographers around the world are taking photos similar to my own, which appear throughout this book.

Pan and the nature spirits, along with all manner of other unseen light beings, are willing to help us connect with nature and assist us in our service to the planet. We may ask for their guidance about how we can cooperate with them as we grow our gardens, build our dwellings, and move through their domains and also in accessing the profound intelligence that interpenetrates all nature.

Meeting Goddess

Goddess is the divine feminine force from which all creation emerges, both here on earth and throughout the cosmos. Goddess is awakening in our hearts and minds, and our DNA is becoming more imbued with spirit as we move from the Age of Pisces and duality to the Age of Aquarius and oneness.

Goddess is revered in nature, homes, temples, ashrams, churches, sacred sites, and deep within our own hearts. She is nature, the land, the sky, the waterways, and the stars. Since the very beginning of civilisation and down through the ages, Goddess has been represented in a profusion of archetypes in stories, paintings, sculptures, carvings, and in song.

The sublime creative power of Goddess is known in indigenous teachings, mystery schools, in various spiritualities and religions by names such as Mother, Mother of Creation, Great Goddess, and the Divine Mother. As the most powerful being in the cosmos she assists us in turning the unknown into the known.

Mother Earth is approaching a 26,000-year cosmic cycle with an alignment with the galactic equator on the solstice of December 21, 2012. As we move towards an event horizon of what many are calling zero point or singularity, the divine feminine and the divine masculine within are naturally and simultaneously uniting in balance and harmony.

Under the loving guidance and influence of Goddess, unprecedented cosmic configurations are awakening us at a very deep cellular, energetic, and spiritual level. We are literally becoming luminous humans by absorbing and integrating more light, and the frequency or vibratory rate of our bodies is quickening to be more in alignment with those in spirit.

These profound inner changes that are spiritualising matter are causing a massive evolution of awareness in humanity, and only time will tell what the new conscious human will create.

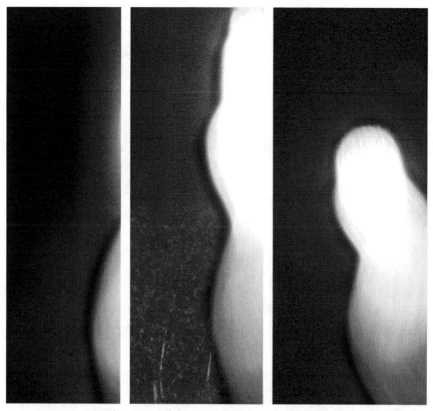

Glimpses of the Goddess of the Gardens

Though it may be accurate to say that Goddess as creator is in every photo I have ever taken, I was honoured to photograph an encounter with an apparition of her in 2008. I was awoken around 2:00 a.m. on a cold, winter morning by a distinct feeling that a holy presence was wishing to commune with me. I hastily pulled on some warm clothes, collected my trusty camera, and followed my inner guidance to the rose garden.

When I reached the garden, I witnessed a glowing luminosity gently showing herself at the very edge of the screen of my camera, and I took a series of approximately twenty photos. The energy of this being felt gentle yet strong, loving, and maternal. She hovered close to me and seemed to be about eighteen feet tall. It was clear by her cautious approach that she was being extra careful not to frighten me.

The exquisite feeling that exuded from her presence was one of overwhelming love and tenderness. Nevertheless, I was still a little afraid while telepathically inviting her to reveal more of herself. She responded to my invitation, no more and no less, and although I later felt that in my anxiety and excitement I had missed having more meaningful communications, I know that I was changed forever by this remarkable meeting. Her presence seemed to recalibrate my energies, and I have no doubt that she opened me to a greater interest in exploring more of the mystery of the divine feminine.

GODDESS ARCHETYPES FROM VARIOUS TRADITIONS

What follows is a small selection of goddess archetypes from a variety of ancient traditions, demonstrating the similarities in the expression of the divine feminine through many diverse cultures.

The Spirit of Quan Yin
Gifted to me by Kinsley Jarrett

Amaterasu (Japanese)—Great goddess of the sun

Anastasia (Russian)—Nature, mystic, cosmic memory, enlightened human

Aphrodite (Greek) and Venus (Roman)—Love, fertility, beauty

Artemis (Greek) and Diana (Roman)—Moon, fertility, childbirth

Asherah (Hebrew)—Mother goddess

Athena (Greek) and Minerva (Roman)—Prudent war, wisdom and domestic crafts

Cerridwen (Celtic)—Magic, wisdom, rebirth, creative inspiration, nature

Demeter (Greek) and Ceres (Roman)—The perfect balance, life and death, love and sorrow

Freya (Norse)—Love, beauty, fertility, war, wealth, divination

Gaia (Greek) and Terra (Roman)—Mother Earth, nature

Green Tara (Buddhist)—Bodhisattva of enlightened activity

Hathor (Egyptian)—Joy, music, dance, fertility, birth, motherhood

Hecate (Greek)—Wild places, childbirth, the crossroads

Ishtar (Semitic) and Inanna (Sumerian)—Goddess self, morning and evening star

Isis (Egyptian)—Healing, power, life, magic, sovereignty

Ixazalvoh (Mayan)—Weaving, female sexuality, childbirth, healer, orator

Kali (Hindu)—Eternal energy, fertility, death, regeneration, change

Lakshmi (Hindu)—Good fortune, wealth, joy, love, peace

Maat (Egyptian)—Truth, justice, balance

Mahatara Great Tara (Buddhist)—Creatrix and mother of all the buddhas and bodhisattvas

Mary Magdalene (Christian)—Partnership, inner strength, wisdom

Morrigan (Celtic)—Warrior, champion of the downtrodden, seer, shape-shifter

Mother Mary (Christian)—Integrity, strength of character, nurturing

Nut (Egyptian)—Afterlife, water, sun, stars, the celestial cycle

Quan Yin (Buddhist)—Compassion, unconditional love

Selena (Greek) and Luna (Roman)—Moon

Shekinah (Hebrew)—Holy Spirit

Sophia (Greek)—Wisdom incarnate

Saraswati (Hindu)—Knowledge, the arts

White Tara (Buddhist)—Compassion, long life, healing, serenity

GOD ARCHETYPES FROM VARIOUS TRADITIONS

In the realm of both mythology and matter, the divine masculine and the divine feminine come to us as archetypes reflected in our day-to-day experiences as impulses, dreams, interests, thoughts, emotions, and synchronicities that offer opportunities to discover more about ourselves.

What follows is a small selection of god archetypes from a variety of ancient traditions, demonstrating the similarities in the expression of the divine masculine through many diverse cultures.

An (Sumerian)—Heaven

Apollo (Greek and Roman)—Light, truth, sun, musician, archer, healer, prophecy

Ares (Greek) and Mars (Roman)—War

Buddha (Buddhist)—Contentment, compassion

Cernunnos (Celtic)—Virility, fertility, life, animals, forests, the underworld

Dionysus (Greek) and Bacchus (Roman)—Wine and vegetation

Enki (Sumerian)—Water, earth, and wisdom

Enlil (Sumerian)—Wind, air, and storms

Eros (Greek) and Cupid (Roman)—Love

Hades (Greek)—God of the Underworld and riches, harsh, reclusive

Hermes (Greek) and Mercury (Roman)—Messenger of the gods to humans

Krishna (Hindu)—Love

Pan (Greek and Pagan)—Nature, creativity, music, poetry, sensuality, and sexuality

Quetzalcoatl (Mesoamerican)—Creator, feathered serpent, intelligence, self-reflection

Ra (Egyptian)—Sun

Rainbow Serpent (Aboriginal)—Land, water, life, social relationships, fertility

The Green Man (Pagan)—Life energy, vegetation, plants, and forests

Wakan Tanka (Lakota Sioux)—Great Spirit

Zeus (Greek) and Jupiter (Roman)—Lord of the sky and supreme ruler of the gods

Pan – The God of Nature

Pan is the grand master of the natural world, who oversees the complex activity of nature on Mother Earth. He embraces nature in its entirety from the smallest elf to the largest sky spirit and from the tiniest flower to the ancient giant redwood. It is virtually impossible for the human mind to comprehend his colossal power.

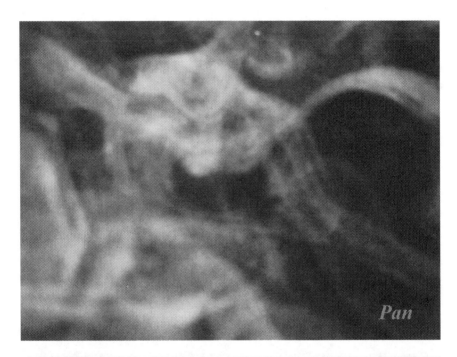

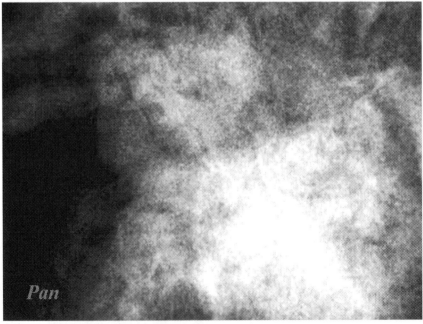

Pan provides a conduit for connecting to the intricate design of nature. He is a multilevel being combining the fully realised abilities of both humans and animals. And in order to relate to us, he may take on the archetypal form of half man and half goat. As the spirit of nature, Pan manifests in ethereal matter, and as is true for all nature spirits, he can morph and change in appearance. He typically appears about twenty feet tall or taller. His torso and head are male, and he has a goatee and horns and the shaggy legs and cloven hoofs of a goat. On occasion, he may be seen playing a flute or pan pipes. Some clairvoyant forest trekkers have reported seeing him sitting on a rock or a log and hearing his laughter or music echoing through the forest. To the mindful observer, his presence may even be recognised as a strong mist of energy, accompanied by an unmistakeably pungent, earthy smell. His magnificent power is definitely not to be underestimated.

Pan shape-shifting into form.

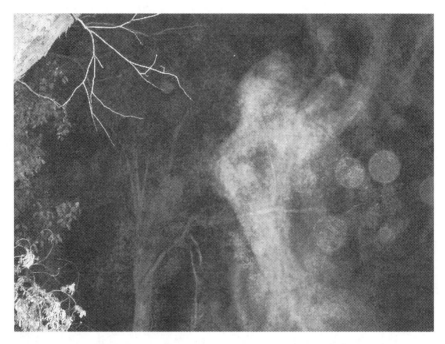

One evening, and not unusually, I felt a strong call to go into the garden. As I became quietly observant, I smelt the familiar earthy and pungent smell that I have come to know as the presence of Pan. I watched in awe as a huge mist swiftly swirled into this classic representation of Pan, inviting me to photograph him before he became mist once more.

THE GREEN MAN

The Green Man is also known as the Old Man of the Woods and the Lord of the Trees. He represents the spirits of trees and plants. He is the subject of sculptures and engravings on churches and cathedrals and appears as a gargoyle on buildings throughout the world, predominantly throughout Europe.

He is usually depicted as a wild man of nature with a very square jaw and hair and beard made of leaves and foliage. He is sometimes seen wearing a floppy hat. His natural mysticism is celebrated throughout the world at earth-honouring festivals.

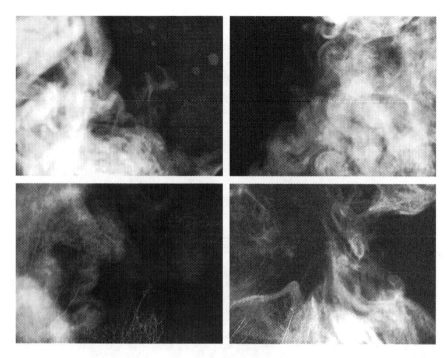

Along with Pan, the Green Man has a profound reverence for Mother Earth and supports humankind in creating a deep connection to more fully understand her sacred mysteries. As guardian for Mother Earth, the Green Man represents the divine masculine or balanced masculine energies, and his modern renaissance encourages men in particular to explore their own manhood and inner harmony and divinity.

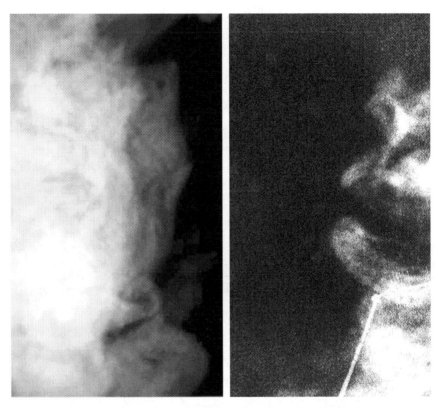

There are a number of fascinating features in my photographs of the Green Man. He consistently shows up with a strong presence, often with leaves forming his hair and his square jaw evident. This assures us that he is not only a man of mythology; he is as real as you and me and is just one of the infinite number of spirit beings who share the environment with us.

GNOMES

This little gnome was wandering around the garden near my studio late one night. He was about two feet tall, and although he seemed shy, he allowed me to photograph him as he continued about his activities.

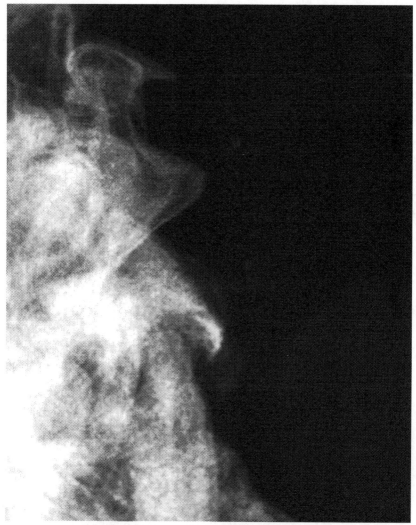

When you are open to us, you will see us.

Many etheric beings frequently inhabit the dominant spirit form. A closer examination of this gnome's perky cap reveals other little entities hitching a ride. Etheric beings, including nature spirits, sometimes also attach themselves to the auras of humans and animals.

Gnomes use the same ephemeral substance that they are created from to enliven the roots of a plant to help it grow. They have families and work harmoniously within their own well-organised societies.

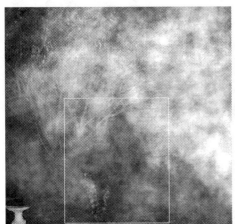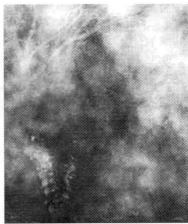

Gnome wearing long leggings, tunic and cap.

Gnomes are intuitive by nature and have difficulty with left-brain logic and the negativity of so many humans. They permeate third-dimensional reality and can travel through stones, rocks, and metals without any resistance. Some also enjoy getting a little tipsy by consuming fermented berries and fruits.

Nature spirits, including gnomes, anchor cosmic forces by receiving energies from the moon and the sun and imprints from stars that filter through them and into the earth. Bringing light to darkness is an essential job. Humans can also assist Mother Earth by consciously anchoring cosmic energies and light.

Gnomes travel to exotic faraway places.

Infinity Orb intrigued by Bruno Torf's flautist gnome.

Breastplate, portal and Spirit Orbs

Beings of the invisible realms love a really dynamic storm. I photographed this breastplate, portal, and spirit orbs during a particularly wild and windy night. Gnomes sometimes wear armoury like this on such stormy occasions. It took a great deal of manoeuvring to keep my camera dry. However, the results were quite unique and well worth the effort.

PIXIES

Pixies, fairies, elves, gnomes, sprites, and other nature spirits are multidimensional beings who may sometimes be seen as orbs and vortices of light. When we view them with our heightened vision, they may also appear holographic, transparent, and humanoid. We may learn about their exceptional magical abilities as we study the vast variety of nature spirits including the tiny winged pixies that sprinkle "pixie dust" to help make things in nature grow.

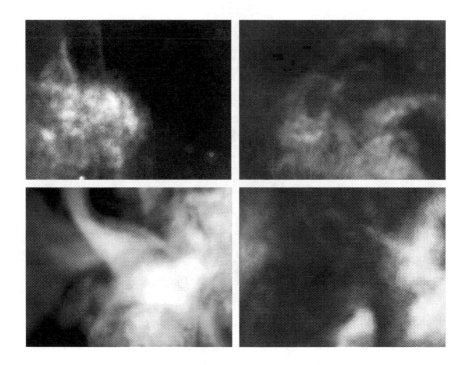

ELVES

Writers such as William Shakespeare, JRR Tolkien, the Brothers Grimm, and JK Rowling have richly discussed the elven, elfish, or elfin worlds in their stories and mythology. Elves, or the "hidden folk," are diminutive humanoids of the etheric realms who demonstrate the light and dark polarities of existence, much as humans do. They live very long lives and some may well even be immortal. The elves of light are known as industrious little helpers and lovers of nature, singing, merriment, and dancing.

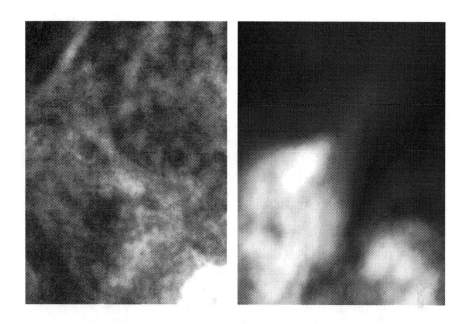

PRIVATE DOMAINS

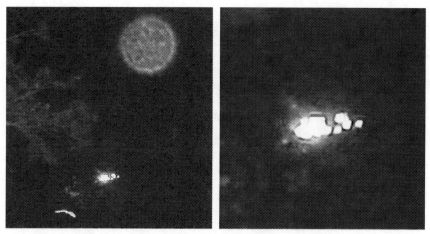

Encountering other-worldly lights in the forest.

 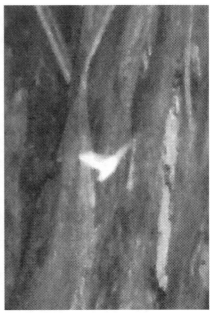

Spirit Animals

Animals are wonderful teachers if we have the sensitivity to observe and connect with them in this manner. I have been aware of different spirit animals and power animals accompanying me throughout my life as mentors, guides, and protectors.

I have only labeled their dominant forms in the photos that follow, and on close study, you will find all other beings in the misty forms.

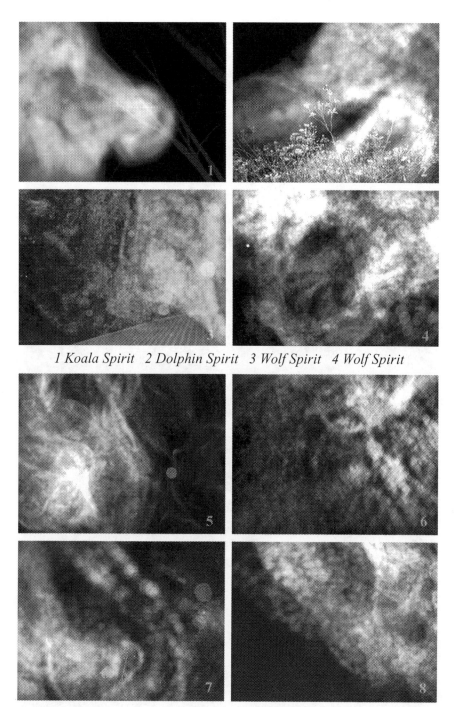

1 Koala Spirit   2 Dolphin Spirit   3 Wolf Spirit   4 Wolf Spirit

5 Feline Spirit   6 Men and Feline Spirits   7 Snake Spirit   8 Snake Spirit

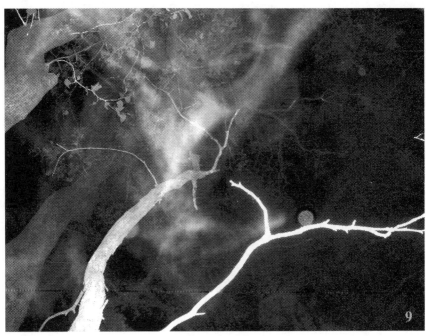

Dragon Spirit

AIR

FAIRIES

Throughout history, human beings have been intensely interested in these tiny beings of light, and many photographs, books, paintings, movies, and costume parties feature their delightful antics. Fairies may also appear in our dreams.

Many adults, as well as children, know that fairies are real, and some tell of their magical encounters with these beings. It is now time for us to more closely examine their cultures, the roles they perform, and how we may connect with them in their work and play. It is respectful to give thanks for all they do and to find ceremonial ways to gift them with sacred offerings.

Large Orb highlights Fairy.

The spirit orbs that accompany me often alert me to interesting activity in the invisible realms. They work in concert with my intuition, which I feel as a warm and tingling sensation in my solar plexus. I have learned to take this feeling as a signal to collect my camera and allow the spirit orbs to take the lead. I would not have photographed this divine fairy in flight had I not been alerted in this way.

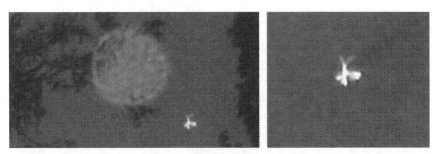

Spirit Orb highlights Fairy.

Full Moon Fairy.

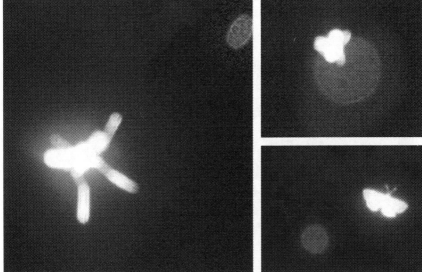

Large Orb highlights Fairy.

CELESTIAL INSECT BEINGS

Insects often get a bad rap, yet where would we be without insects such as bees, flies, and silkworms? What would pollinate our plants, break down what is no longer living, and provide the finest of threads for weaving exquisite cloth?

There is also a teeming world of celestial insect beings in the invisible realms that hold, as yet, untold secrets about healing and helping.

ANGELIC PRESENCES

Angels are featured in all religions and spiritual traditions as comforters, guides, protectors, and assistants. Over the years, I have experienced their presence numerous times, most often when in the face of danger or in need of comfort or inspiration.

In the early days of writing The New Frontier, I was having difficulty finding a way to present my photographs, so I took myself to the forest and sat on a rock by the creek and simply asked for an appropriate framework. To my sheer delight, the unseens showed how I could honour the five elements and some of the other fascinating phenomena that I have photographed.

I also recognized the assistance of angels at those times when "someone" prevented me from stepping into the path of a speeding truck, when I received comfort in intensive care while I hovered between life and death, during gruelling inner work, and when making all manner of decisions both large and small.

Clouds often imbue the presence of angelic spirits. I have seen marvellous photos by others on the Internet and in books of wonderful light beings that appear to be from the angelic realms. However, the presence of angels come to me as hints in clouds, while others come as spirit orbs, which I intuitively recognize as angelic.

In early 2011, I went to the beach to contemplate a major life decision and to ask spirit for help. I was fascinated when I saw this cloud forming. As I tuned into its presence, I was astonished to see it brighten and then flash a luminescence, indicating some kind of intelligence. The feeling was definitely angelic, and interestingly, I instantly found the clarity and direction I needed to relocate for my greater well-being.

Sylphs

Sylphs are spiritual beings of the element air and are seen in these photos moving at great speed and enjoying the wind. They can be tiny or so immense that they span the sky and interpenetrate the earth. They move very quickly over vast distances in their role of detoxifying the air.

Sylphs are associated with all things of the sky and air, including the very air we breathe. Call on them for inspiration and for healing of all kinds, particularly for any respiratory complaints.

LOOK TO THE SPACES

In the early 1990s, I was fortunate to spend a lot of time with a dear friend Kinsley Jarrett, who has since passed over to the spirit worlds. Kinsley was a remarkable man who had a great love for all life in the natural world. He also had exceptional abilities as a musician and as a clairvoyant, visionary artist who worked swiftly in very fine detail.

Kinsley had a particular affinity with Pan, and he also communed with and illustrated all manner of nature spirits, along with extraterrestrials or galactics and celestials, such as archangels, ascended masters, and spirit guides. He brought wisdom and solace to others with his skill in automatic writing and channelled messages from the spirit worlds. I have been aware of his presence and support throughout this writing, as he was very aligned to this subject matter.

Over the years, Kinsley and I shared many joyous experiences together in nature, and I once asked him if he would teach me to see the way that he did. As always, he was patient with me and quietly said, "You are looking at what is obvious. Look at what is not there. Look to the spaces."

I took this photograph the morning after a friend and dedicated Japanologist came to dinner. He has an all-abiding interest in traditional Japanese culture, literature, antiquities, and ritual. Prior to dinner, my friend and I walked through the splendid gardens of my home at the time, and he related details of his discoveries and rituals during his recent trip to Japan and of how he was building a Japanese teahouse in his own garden.

I invite you to soften your gaze and look to the spaces. Half close your eyes if that helps. Clear your mind of thoughts. What do you feel and see? What do you instinctively know? As with all things, the ability to connect with spirits increases with focus and the willingness to allow what is there to emerge, rather than to anticipate an outcome by having certain expectations.

Soft eye focus reveals what resides in the spaces.

I see a Zen master blessing a woman in a long dress and also other forms in the photograph. Are we accessing different timelines in the quantum field? Are these holographic apparitions of the spirits of my friends and my own combined interests? Are they aspects of us or of our past or future lives?

When we begin seeing in new ways, images start leaping out of bathroom tiles and patterned fabric. Number plates on cars become meaningful or humourous. We turn on the radio just in time to hear the answer to our question in a song. The clock says, "Notice everything," when it displays double and triple numbers such as 11:11, 3:33, and 5:55. Shapes of animals and angels take form in clouds and trees, and we become more aware of the synchronicities and what are, no doubt, miracles in our lives.

FIRE

SALAMANDERS

Salamanders are fire elementals that often resemble large butterflies, dragons, or humans with wings. These spiritual beings create the sparks of life for fires and gather light to anchor into Mother Earth, which helps awaken other beings.

We can assist the many trillions of spirits of nature by becoming aware of their activities and co-creating with them in their selfless service of sustaining nature.

Have you ever felt you have company when gazing into an open fire? You do.

Salamanders are Fire Elementals.

WATER

UNDINES

As with all elemental beings, the undines are evolved souls who may live for many hundreds of years. Their domain is water, and they can be called upon for healing and safety with all things concerning water, including the rivers, oceans, waterfalls, lakes, and even the water we drink.

Undines are Water Elementals that love frolicking in the rain.

Call on the Undines to help cleanse the waterways.

ETHER

ETHERIC MULTIDIMENSIONALS

This fifth section addresses those ephemeral or spirit beings not necessarily related to the first four elements. Extraterrestrials or galactics sometimes appear in my photos, along with what I now know to be intraterrestrials or inner-earth beings.

I coined the term *etherics* and collectively call these spirit beings either multidimensionals or etherics. Some etherics may even be my own thought forms. Some are humanoid, while others are unusual, and some are so immense that I am able to only photograph a small portion of their bodies. As with many of these mysterious life forms, other beings often inhabit the same substance.

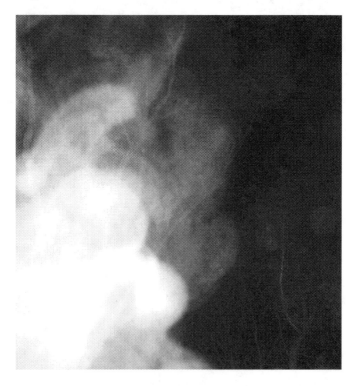

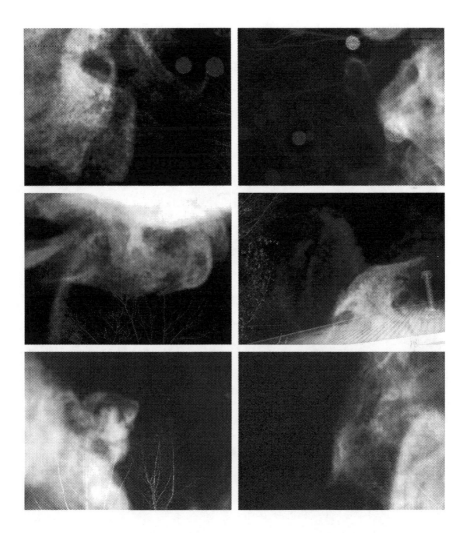

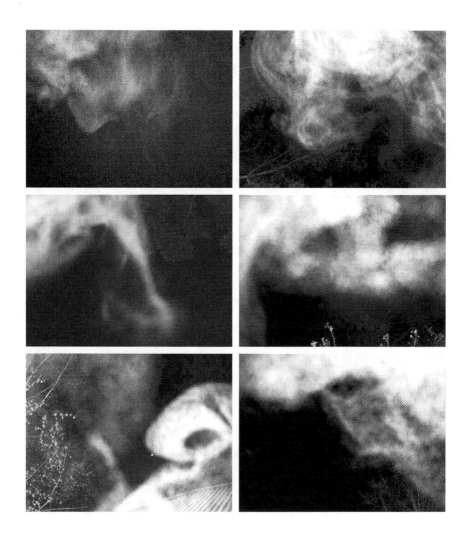

CONFUSED SPIRITS

Some spirits, just like some humans, are confused and blocked in their development. Like humans, these spirits have good reasons for this, as they may have suffered dreadful treatment at times in their lives. If you become aware of any earthbound and confused spirits, you can help them release their attachment to the earthly realms by extending loving kindness and encouraging them to move to the safety of the sacred light.

Like attracts like, whether human or in spirit, and therefore, our wholeness or woundedness attracts us to others of a similar vibrational energy of evolutionary development. Psychologically and alchemically, we can transform all challenging feelings and turn our pain into understanding and empathy, betrayal into forgiveness, loneliness into companionship, sadness into joy, meanness into generosity, and fear into love.

Earthbound Spirits around an historic church.

AGGRESSIVE SPIRITS

There are also mischievous and ghoulish beings in the spirit worlds. Negative spirits are parasitic and may give you a feeling of queasiness in your solar plexus and chest or a general feeling of apprehension. Always trust your feelings and instincts, as they will never let you down.

I have many photographs of these entities and have chosen not to publish any, as their darkness is too pervasive and disturbing to circulate. Similarly, I do not recommend dabbling in seances, ghost hunting, or watching horror movies, as it is all too easy to call in negative and aggressive spirits. They feed off people's fears, weaknesses, shame, guilt, addictions, and bad habits. Greedy spirits often attach themselves to people, eventually making them sick or addicted.

It is a good idea to decide how you will deal with negative entities if you ever encounter them. I choose not to entertain them at all, and as they dislike direct attention, I define very strong boundaries by surrounding myself with bright light and verbally or telepathically demanding them to disappear and never return.

Therefore, I recommend moving them out of your space by being very firm and sending a strong and convincing statement, such as, "Only entities of positive and loving intent are welcome in my life." This, by the way, holds good for humans too. Skillful spiritual healers know how to remove these entities and the debilitating effects of their attachment.

Be sure to clear your space when you sense or see that the negatives have left. You can raise the vibrations of your environment with beautiful music, chanting, cleaning, loving intention, and smudging by burning dried herbs and white sage, sweetgrass and cedar for their purifying smoke. You may also call upon the guardian forces of benevolent extraterrestrials, power animals, guides, ascended masters, and angels to help and protect you.

"Be a Tree" Meditation

This meditation is designed to help you get in touch with the oneness of nature and to assist you in finding personal stability, harmony, and balance. You will be guided to metaphorically feel the experience of being a strong and majestic tree, and you may even meet some of the types of elementals discussed here in part one.

You may like to read the meditation onto a recording device or have someone read it to you, being sure to allow plenty of time to be fully immersed in the experience. Repeat this meditation as often as you wish. Find a beautiful place in nature to sit, resting against the trunk of a tree or in your meditation sanctuary or meditation group.

Close your eyes and take three deep, relaxing breaths right into the core of your belly and exhale them gently through the cells of your entire body.

Watch your belly expand as you breathe in and your body open and relax as you breathe out.

Breathe in.

Breathe out.

Notice the sounds of nature around you.

Peaceful.

Inviting.

Visualize a magnificent tree before you.

Hear it whisper something to you as you approach it.

Feel the texture and smell the fragrance of the tree.

Now with one deep relaxing breath, allow yourself to merge into the centre of the majestic tree, and in your imagination, rise to enable your body to gracefully fill the trunk of the tree.

Feel your feet, legs and the base of your spine sinking deep, deep, deep into Mother Earth down, down into the moist, dark ground to become one strong and stable taproot.

Watch as your feet and legs branch out to create a far-reaching labyrinth of finer roots.

Your head stretches and expands to occupy a dynamic space amongst the foliage, and you feel a whole new level of perfect clarity and acute perception.

Your hands and arms rise as they transform into many strong and intricate branches.

Watch as vibrant leaves sprout on your network of branches and twigs reaching into the sky.

Sublime cosmic forces and information enter your being.

Become aware that you are a conduit of light, absorbing sunlight and starlight.

As you anchor this light into the ground, know that you are literally anchoring heaven on earth.

Stretch your entire being luxuriously and fully inhabit your new identity as a dignified tree.

Feel your perfect balance, stability, and harmony.

Be flexible like the tree in the wind.

Observe how it feels to stand strong yet supple like the tree.

Now experience the life within and around you.

Notice what is occurring throughout your entire system.

Begin at the tips of your roots and work up to your trunk and then into your branches, twigs, and leaves. Feel your essence and presence.

Tune in to the interplay of all your aspects and to your connectedness within yourself and the world around you.

Become aware of other trees and how you communicate with them.

You are a reservoir of wisdom and have many lessons to teach and stories to tell.

Each tree ring is a year's storehouse of growth with every full cycle of the sun.

Tap into the knowledge archived in each of your rings.

What do you teach of the changing of the seasons, of the gifts of abundance, of giving and receiving, sheltering, patience, beauty, freedom, mystery, and generosity to visitors over the years of your life?

Observe all the life forms that you shelter and nourish—birds, bugs, bees, butterflies and other insects and wildlife.

Listen to the harmonious sounds of life within and around you.

Soften your inner sight to become aware of those who dwell in your subtle places and spaces—transparent elemental beings like devas, fairies, gnomes, pixies, and elves.

Feel the spirit of your tree.

Tune into tree consciousness.

Identify the feeling.

How long has your tree resided here?

What is it capable of?

What does it know?

Listen deeply within.

There is profound ancient wisdom in this tree.

It has a personal message for you.

What does it want you to know?

Take some time to fully absorb this message.

Now thank the tree for all its gifts.

When you are ready, slowly withdraw your consciousness back from every part of the tree.

Draw yourself out of the roots.

Come back up from the ground, and back from the branches, leaves, and trunk.

Allow the tree to send you safely back into your body—back home to yourself.

Return fully and totally into your body.

Breathe naturally and begin to move.

Notice the sounds around you and become aware of your breathing.

Recall your personal message from the tree and reflect upon it.

Open your eyes and gently complete your meditation.

Spirits of the Tree

I know this stately tree well and have spent many wonderful hours in its company. I have also taken many photographs of it in its various moods and seasons. One bright, sunny day I was surprised to find "faces" in the trunk and branches and then, on some occasions at night, to see very active spirit orbs around it.

Spirits of the tree by night.

Spirits of the tree by day.

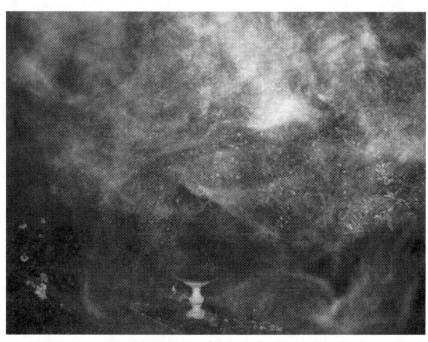

The Spirits of the Apple Tree.

How to Photograph Spirits

Most days and nights, I delight in photographing and interacting with the spirit orbs, elementals and other spirits of the unseen realms. I am as interested now as I was in the beginning of my journey.

When we start on this adventure with spirit beings, the journey deepens and reveals more according to our interest in integrating the information and whether we have the curiosity to explore further. People all over the world who are photographing similar phenomena frequently contact me via Facebook and my websites to share their personal photos, stories, and discoveries.

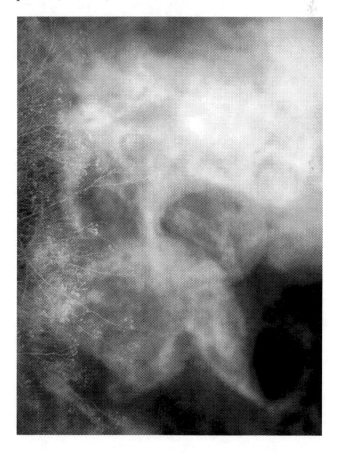

It is very gratifying to help others take their own photographs of life in the multidimensional realms. I delight in introducing them to these worlds, being in their wonder as they connect, and answering their questions if I possibly can. Each person finds his or her own unique method, and here are some suggestions that work for me that may help you too.

Approach spirit beings, including orbs, with curiosity
and open-mindedness.

❋

Be receptive and resourceful and have a respectful manner.
Sing and talk to them.

❋

Fully participate by inviting them to reveal themselves
and interact with them.

❋

Joyfulness and playfulness work wonders, so have fun
with your adventures.

❋

Use either a video camera or a simple digital camera,
preferably with the flash turned on.

❋

Photograph spirits during the day or night, either
indoors or outdoors.

❋

Express gratitude by greeting them when they show up and
thanking them when they leave.

❋

Spirits love celebrations, musical events, animals, nature,
children, and storms, so film there.

❋

Establish telepathic communications with the spirit orbs
and other spirit beings.

◉

Go beyond the "wow factor" by planning questions and
getting to know "regulars."

◉

Watch your language. It is disrespectful to "shoot,"
"capture," or "hunt" spirit beings.

◉

Observe their movement on the screen of your camera
by half depressing the shutter.

◉

Watch your pet's line of sight and point your camera to
the focus of the animal's interest.

◉

Study your photos on your computer screen, as the
light enhances intricate details.

◉

Always save your originals and work from a copy
when adjusting the brightness and size.

◉

Delve deeper by communicating with the spirits that visit you.

◉

Share your photos in books, videos, exhibitions,
presentations, and on social media.

◉

Share your discoveries with others only if they express
a genuine interest.

◉

Show the same respect as you would to an honoured
guest in your home.

◉

Be positive and open to the ongoing wonders that still
await you in the spirit worlds.

◉

Follow the line of sight of your pet's fascination.

I believe this brief photographic coverage of some of the elementals
in the unseen realms unequivocally proves their existence. Prior to
this type of photography, there was much conjecture about nature
spirits and spirit beings. Those who saw fairies, gnomes, elves, and
angels were often derided, and ongoing debate continued for centuries
in many private circles, as well as in the mainstream media.

There are, perhaps, millions of people of all ages now photographing elementals, spirit orbs, celestials, galactics, ascended masters, and other spirit beings. These spirit beings have been with us all along, and fortunately, we now have the opportunity to delve deeper and to work in cooperation with these enlightened wise ones for the good of all and for the well-being of Mother Earth.

PART TWO

Fascinating Phenomena
of the Unseen Realms

*Spirit Orbs where my sister and I had been in
conversation earlier that day.*

In conversation

SPIRIT ORBS: MY CONSTANT COMPANIONS

From the very beginning of photographing life in the spirit worlds, I found it curious that eight specific orbs showed up in many of my photos. I named the three most active ones Infinity, Wonky the Wise, and Bright One. I refer to these eight orbs as my "constant companions," and they may be associated with an octave or eight aspects of my multidimensionality.

Photographing the aura   *Finer multidimensional aspects*

My Spirit Team

Infinity

A beautiful shiny orb with the characteristic infinity symbol along with other unique features often turns up in photos of me at my upper left at about forty-five degrees. Sometimes Infinity appears as a ray of light entering the left side of my head, and as it transmits information I feel a very pleasant tingling sensation in my head.

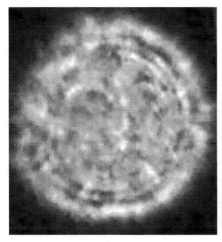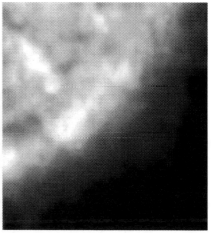

Infinity is a focus for accessing my akashic records.

Infinity is always well framed in the photos, regardless of where I travel and where I point my camera. I feel profound peace and very blessed whenever it appears.

Over time, I intuitively came to know that Infinity was guiding and teaching me. I discovered that the spirit orbs are actually soul carriers, light vehicles, or Merkabahs and that Infinity acts as a vehicle for my higher unlimited self.

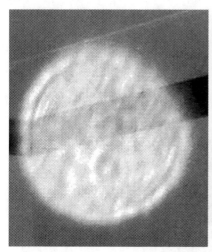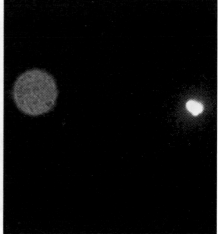

The higher unlimited self is the multidimensional wholeness and eternal oversoul that guides us to our highest potential. It is the totality of who we have been, who we are, and who we are becoming.

Meditation, stillness, prayer, observing dreams, and mindfulness in nature are just some of the ways to connect with the higher self.

Using soft focus to study the first photograph, I started seeing images of different people working at a variety of professions, and in a luminous flash of realisation, I understood that I was reading my own akashic records. Miraculously, this orb was demonstrating the journey of my soul through various timelines.

The bands and the outer rings of colour seem to relate to the frequencies of the many finer vibrational dimensions. By imagining the two-dimensional circle as an orb or a ball or sphere of light and spinning it, it is easy to see it as a very efficient vehicle for travel.

In 2010, I joined in experiments with friends where we projected our orb or soul selves at a prearranged time, and to our delight, Infinity showed up in some of their photos and their personal orbs showed in mine. Occasionally, Infinity has visited close friends of its own volition as seen in their photographs.

Infinity Orb is a vortex for Soul travel.

Infinity Orb is also a vortex or tunnel of vibrancy, as seen in these three photos. The tunnel is coded with information that reveals our essential nature, as well as providing access to the mystery.

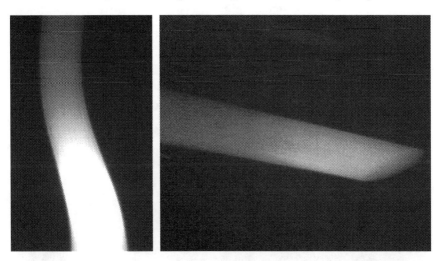

Moving in day.

Wonky the Wise

This spirit orb knows when I am about to take a photo even before my conscious self does. It always frames itself in the upper right of the photo whenever it decides to show up. When tuning in to its protective presence, I feel that Wonky is my angelic self or guardian angel. Thankfully, it doesn't seem to mind the rather irreverent name I have bestowed upon it. I have only to look around me at these many spirit orbs to know that I am never alone.

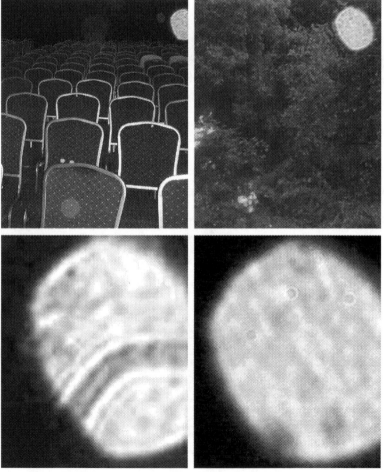

Wonky the Wise prefers the upper right of my photographs.

BRIGHT ONE

Bright One is a shiny, playful, and inquisitive large orb. It delights in leading the way and gets into all sorts of humorous antics. Bright One also responds to my telepathic suggestions of where to place itself in the landscape.

Bright One is a shiny playful Orb.

Although there are now many books, websites, and videos with information about spirit orbs, I feel the studies of this phenomenon, including my own observations, are still very much in their fledgling stages. I believe we have much to learn from and about them, and in time, our interactions will become second nature and whole new worlds will open to us.

Playtime with Spirit Orbs

Spirit Orbs with my sister Chris Hooper and Didi the dog.

I wonder if I can juggle Orbs?

Spirit Orbs with the Celtic Prayer Flags

Spirit Orbs are my travelling companions.

Infinity Orb admires rocket man the roof.

Iridescent blue Orb watches the fire twirling.

In the company of Golden Light.

Preparing for the 11:11:11 group meditation.

Anastasia's Sphere of Light

Anastasia is a goddess of nature, enlightened visionary, and teacher. Her life and methods are the subject of ten books in the Ringing Cedars Series written by Russian author Vladimir Megre.

Anastasia was orphaned as an infant and left to survive largely on her own in the cedar forests of Siberia. Growing up in this way in the pristine forest, she developed the enhanced attributes of a fully realised human. She models the optimal or future human by having mastered instant manifestation, creative imagery, psychic abilities, bilocation, time travel, enlightened consciousness, and being at one with nature.

Anastasia's Sphere of Light
Photo credit: Ringing Cedars Publishers

A large sphere of light or spirit orb has been her mentor, companion, and protector from the very beginning. Her spirit orb may also be the vehicle for her multidimensional higher self.

Anastasia's visions for the future and innovative philosophies have inspired millions around the world to put these radiant visions into action. She encourages like-hearted people to attain a hectare of land on which to build their kin's or family's domain, rear their children in love, grow their own food, and live in harmony with nature.

PORTALS TO OTHER DIMENSIONS

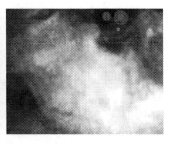

Some earth sensitives and clairvoyants have the ability to experience and see vortices or portals to other realms of existence in a tree or rock face and in well-known sacred power places on earth. Meditators may also discover the small sacred sanctuaries in the high heart and pineal gland to find energy doorways to other realms of existence. Now, interested photographers have the opportunity to explore portals to other worlds too.

I focused on a pier in a picturesque fishing village in Australia with the Pacific Ocean in the background. This result was not the scene I expected. Infinity Orb is in the foreground of what I believe to be a portal or wormhole to another realm.

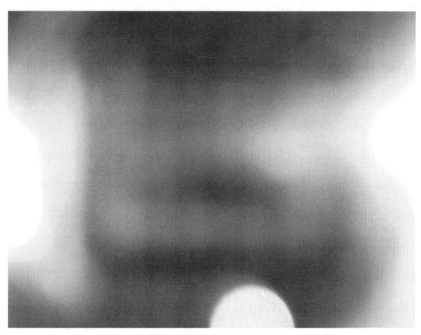

Portal to other realms.

UNIDENTIFIED FLYING OBJECTS

Quite often unidentified flying objects, or UFOs, appear in my photos, and as yet I have no accurate idea as to who or what they are. Frequently, what many refer to as UFOs are actually identifiable as spacecraft.

UFO in the forest

Infinity observes UFO

Infinity Orb is curious about all the phenomena in the unseen realms and often highlights things of interest in my photos. The small UFO in the second photo near the birch trees was impossible to miss due to its energy and brightness. It was photographed during a storm, and the tiny lights are raindrops.

 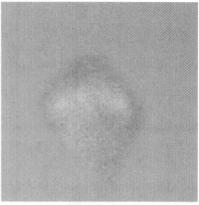

Merkabah shaped UFO　　　　　　*The UFO enhanced*

While driving along a deserted road in New Mexico, I felt a pressing urge to stop the car to take some photographs. It was only later, while viewing all my photos for the day, that I discovered I'd had company on the road.

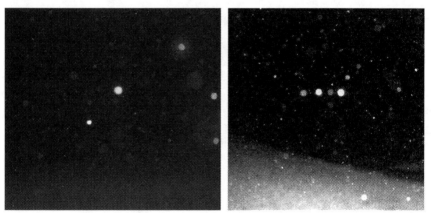

Five brightly coloured lights move into a new formation.

An exquisite full moon rising huge and orange drew me to the beach. My intuition had nudged me to take a series of photos in a panoramic sweep over the ocean. I saw flickering lights change formation over the shallow water close to the beach.

UFO cloaking clouds near Magdalena, New Mexico.

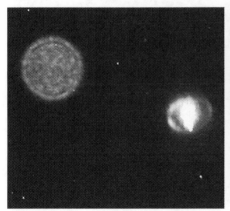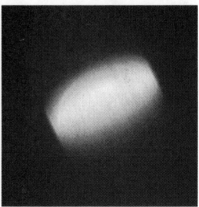

SACRED GEOMETRY

I quite frequently observe spirit orbs making shapes found in sacred geometry—circles, triangles, squares, hexagons, vesica piscis, and the like. At times, they also appear to form starry constellations.

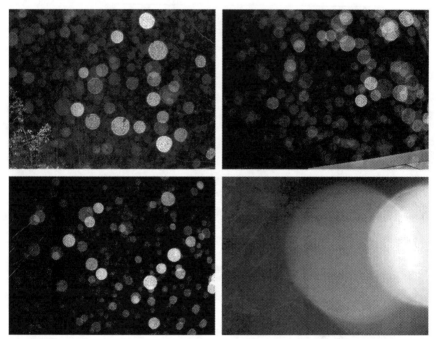

Triangles, Pyramids, Circles, Spheres, Squares, Cubes and Vesica Pisces

Beams of Light

In these photos, we see baby Mali at the Melbourne Zoo still very connected to the world of spirit. She has not yet fully separated into her earthly experience of duality as the mature elephants have. This beam is a spiritual umbilical cord still connecting her to universal source, from where all living things incarnate.

The spiritual umbilical cord is still clearly
connected to the baby elephant.

Beams, rods, and tubes of light contain highly complex light codes and energy, in sets of geometric symbols, sigils and fractals that travel through them into ley lines, life forms, and landscapes. They are, literally, conduits for bringing the divine spirit to earth.

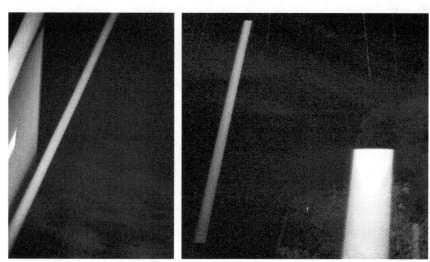

Multidimensional beams of light

Beams of Light anchor highly complex codes of information and energy.

Comprehensive information travels via beams of light. Some beams have the appearance of steel piping. They also frequently appear as white or golden tubes of light and sometimes are in rainbow colours.

RODS

Throughout time, rods have been used for healing, manifesting from the unseen, and communicating information. Rods may also help illumine us with greater consciousness. Indeed, they may be seen as magic wands when used with the skills of finer perception.

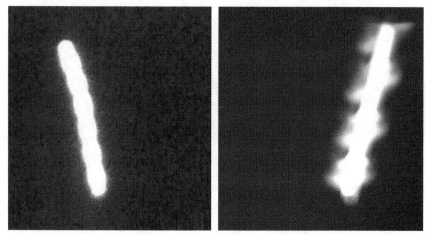

Rods of Light for healing, manifestation and communication.

WE ARE NOT ALONE

Humanoids, animals, and some very unusual life forms appear in many of my photos of life in the unseen realms. I am training myself to learn from these beings and devising suitable protocol to communicate with them. I am curious as to why they appear to some of us and not to others. Perhaps it is because those of us who see them are open, and they sense our goodwill and willingness to form sincere relationships with them.

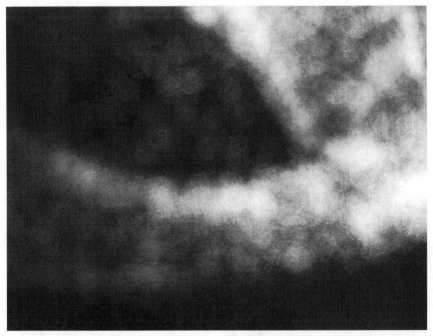

A massive entity peered directly into the lens of the my camera

A vast variety of beings live in the finer frequency realms of earth and beyond. I have friends who have had lifelong interactions with their stellar and/or inner-earth families. Some have been working and co-creating with them, particularly in the areas of technology, healing, and cosmic understanding and in service to Mother Earth.

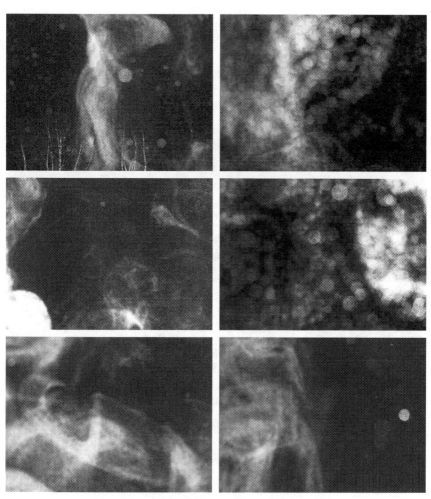

Interdimensional Beings from other realms

ENERGY GRID

We can train our eyes to see the infinite number of bright lights of the vital life force in the landscape and the energy glow around all living things. I created this graphic to show a configuration of how I see the pranic energy grid, which looks to me rather like honeycomb. This can be seen by choosing a segment of sky and then going into a light trance with soft eye focus. Pretty soon, points of energy will appear and twinkle in dynamic moving patterns.

Dynamic energy grid

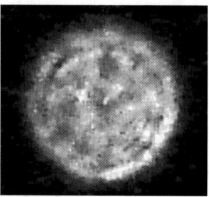

Grid in Orb

Energy Grid photographed at midnight

Window in the Sky

Late one afternoon after a relaxing energy healing, I took a walk on the beach with a friend. To our amazement, we watched as a gap or window appeared in the sky over the ocean and formations in rainbow colours began to reveal a procession of images within this window. Although I didn't have a camera to document this event, the window appeared in the dimensions as shown in this photo.

Memories retrieved from our minds.

Over the hour or more that we observed this phenomenon, it occurred to us that the intelligence behind this had somehow accessed our combined interests and created scenes of the interests and experiences that were meaningful to us. Whales, dolphins, and other wildlife; crop circles, forests, and significant scenes from journeys we had each made; and the nativity, ascended masters, and nature spirits all became a moving slideshow in rainbows.

SACRED AND CELESTIAL MUSIC

Deva Premal and her partner, Miten, spend most of their life travelling the world giving sublime performances to packed auditoriums. Their music, chanting, and satsang circles are an expression of their spiritual devotion that resonates deeply with listeners and participants.

Deva Premal chants sacred music.

Music is expressed in every culture on earth. Countless books have been written about spiritual and religious music, and this section is a very brief acknowledgment of how music, singing, chanting, and toning have the ability to open us to heightened states of consciousness, love, and bliss. The vibrating frequencies in sacred music enable the body and mind to achieve harmony.

Some people gifted with multidimensional listening or clairaudience report hearing the sounds of the universe, which many refer to as the music of the spheres. Some, who are preparing to die, hear this glorious and reassuring music weeks and days before they pass over. Sometimes the music is accompanied by visions of angels and other beings of light.

Nature, animals, and birds also have their music. As we tune into the sounds of the natural world, we come to understand the messages and restorative healing available to all. The symphony of running water, the song of the wind, and the messages in sunshine and moon glow are familiar. It's difficult to imagine a world without the cacophonies of birdsong. As we move into fourth and fifth dimensional living, we will learn to more fully understand the conversations and songs of wildlife such as birds, frogs, whales, dolphins, and wolves.

My friend Kinsley Jarrett, who I introduced in the section "Look to the Spaces," had extraordinary experiences with celestial music and was sometimes able to record it. He shared one of the sessions of music that had recorded itself onto a cassette tape. This phenomenon happened often, and each time, my friend was able to listen to the music on the cassette only three times. I heard the second playing of one such recording. Kinsley placed a chair for me in the middle of four speakers and turned on the tape. I was totally transported by the singing of a celestial choir of what sounded like thousands of exquisite voices, accompanied by the sublime music from hundreds of the finest symphony orchestras. After Kinsley had listened for the third time, the music inexplicably disappeared completely off the tape.

ABORIGINAL SPIRITS

Traditional indigenous people of Australia and elsewhere have maintained their connection to the worlds of spirit by supportive practices designed to keep their extrasensory abilities intact. It appears that the pineal gland, which activates the spiritual eye, begins to atrophy by the age of twelve in most westerners. This is not so in indigenous cultures, which revere connection to the subtle realms of Mother Earth and the spirit worlds, retaining open access to these realms through their oral teachings and practices.

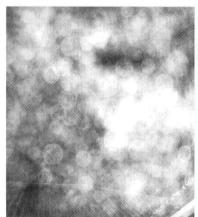

Aboriginal presence

IMAGINATION

Imagination is a multilayered and complex skill of the multidimensional selves. Each aspect of self embellishes the potency and effectiveness of the imagination, and by consciously using it, we strengthen our psychic abilities, creative forces, and genuine connection to the divine.

Notice everything

I sometimes joke that we need seven I's when working to evolve our understanding of life at all levels. These I's are imagination, intuition, impeccability, ideas, intention, inquisitiveness, and interest.

Expand the imagination by rotating some photos.

DO SPIRIT ORBS CREATE CROP CIRCLES?

The appearance of crop circles in fields of grain in many parts of the world has intensified during the past two decades. By far the greatest number of these designs materialise in fields in the Wessex Triangle in southern England beginning around April and culminating prior to the harvest in August. Spirit orbs are frequently photographed in and around these formations and seem to be intricately connected with this phenomenon; indeed, they may even create them.

In 1997, I had the good fortune of being at the Barge Inn, the local hub for croppies in Wiltshire, to see a video filmed by a local farmer showing three light orbs moving over a field on his farm in the early hours of the morning. I watched the video many times and was astonished to see the three small orbs descending and circling over the field three times, leaving a large and intricate design in their wake in just twelve short seconds. There is now a preponderance of evidence by many croppies reporting the link between light orbs and crop circles.

CROP CIRCLES AND GLYPHS

What is this fascinating phenomenon of circles and glyphs that are sometimes to be found in fields of grain and occasionally in sand and snow? Who or what is creating them and why?

The first known reference to a crop circle was depicted in a woodcut in 1678 showing a huge elliptical glyph in a grain crop. While we have reports of these mysterious occurrences throughout our history, we find the circle makers have been particularly active since the Harmonic Convergence in August 1987, mostly in England and, more recently, in other countries including Italy, the Netherlands, the Czech Republic, Russia, and Germany.

The reason for so many glyphs appearing in southern England may have to do with the ten-foot wide energy meridians known as the Michael-Mary ley lines that flow in a straight line through sacred sites such as St Michael's Mount in Cornwall, linking with Stonehenge, the Avebury Stone Circles, and Silbury Hill.

Near Stonehenge 2002   *Near Silbury Hill 2004*
Crop Circle photo credits: Crop Circle Connector.

Theories abound as to who creates these circles or glyphs and why. Researchers studying the geometry, symbology, and creation of the glyphs often differ greatly in their conclusions. Certainly, every season provides opportunities for everyone involved to bring out the very best in him or herself. Surely, the glyphs have the ability to open hearts more and to awaken greater awareness in the people who are drawn to them. Possibly more important though are the encodings received by Mother Earth to help in her recalibration and return to wholeness.

Swallow in ancient artifact.   *Swallows glyph UK 2003*

Some say extraterrestrials or galactics create the glyphs, while others believe they are the work of nature spirits and inner-earth beings. Some insist that humans make them all.

My personal theory is that we are, indeed, the creators, though not by the silly hoax of men or women skulking around the fields at night and stomping on stalks of grain. Rather, we create them at a multidimensional or quantum level of the one mind, from a place beyond time and third-dimensionality, in the realms of unity consciousness where we are human, extraterrestrial, and nature spirit in one.

Eyewitnesses and many video accounts reveal that spheres of light are frequently seen above these fields, creating complex and geometrically precise designs in mere seconds. Supporting this theory are numerous accounts by researchers, either individually or in groups, focusing upon a chosen design, which mysteriously appears in a field of grain soon thereafter.

I have often wondered whether I may also have connected to a similar group intention or stream of consciousness. In 1997, I was led by many remarkable synchronicities from Mt. Shasta in California, to a field in Wiltshire in the United Kingdom, all in less than a week, to have my first momentous experience with a crop circle.

In late 1996, I travelled extensively in a camper van through much of California and the Four Corners region of the United States, and in April 1997, I rented a beautifully located apartment where I could look out to the mysterious mountain at Mt Shasta. I spent my days meditating and researching, meeting the locals, exploring the mountain, and taking photographs of lenticular clouds and landscapes, including the magnificent forests around Lake Siskiyou.

On the US Independence Day, July 4, I watched a series of DVDs with friends during breaks in the celebrations that explored the features of the tube torus, which later led to further studies of sacred geometry, the golden mean, the Fibonacci spiral, the flower of life, the Merkabah, Metatron's Cube, zero point, and the harmonics of sound.

Something ignited in me that day, and on the very next day, I signed off on my apartment and travelled north along the Oregon coast to Portland, where I sold my camper van and boarded an aeroplane for London, not really knowing why I was doing this. I was merely following very strong inner impulses.

On arrival at Heathrow, I rented a car and followed my impulse again, which surprisingly, did not take me to London. Instead, I travelled west. That night, I stayed in a stunning bed and breakfast with a luxurious bath and the best of British humour on the radio.

The following day, I gave free reign to my intuition again. It took me along the M3 to an arts festival in Marlborough, Wiltshire, which meant most of the accommodation was booked out. It was now July 12, 1997. Imagine my surprise when the gentleman giving me directions to a bed and breakfast drew a mud map of country lanes with the key locator being the latest crop circle at Alton Barnes, which was a massive tube torus overlooking one of the twenty-four chalk horses that grace certain grassy slopes and fields throughout Britain.

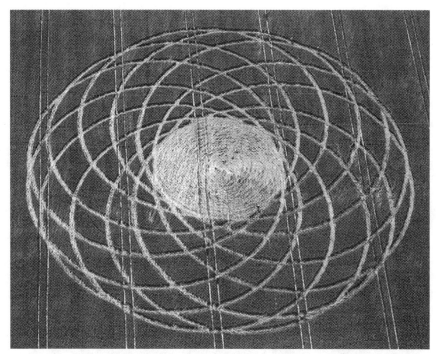

Tube Torus, Alton Barnes near Avebury, Wiltshire 11 July 1997.

The dimensions of the immaculately crafted tube torus may be estimated by the size of the people as seen in the middle of the photo above. That evening, I watched the sun set from the very centre of this crop circle, overlooking an ancient white chalk horse to the left, and before me, I swear the goddess was lying in the field in elegant repose. Thus began my ongoing study of crop circles and the role of the tube torus and its relevance to our understanding of life on earth and throughout the universe.

In February 2008, I attended the seventeenth annual UFO Conference in Laughlin, Nevada, where many of the presenters were researchers of the paranormal whose work I respected and had been studying for some time. Dolores Cannon, David Wilcock, JJ and Desiree Hurtak, Jamie Maussan, and Nancy Talbot were a few among the forty speakers presenting that year.

I was invited to spend a couple of weeks with two other researchers I met at the conference who lived in Roswell, New Mexico. They generously shared much of their own studies, including details about the Roswell UFO incident, the alleged crash of an extraterrestrial spacecraft and the capture of its alien occupants in mid-1947. They took me to the building where they had evidence of the spacecraft having been stored.

My hosts also showed me a stone of unknown origin that was found in the desert near Roswell by their friend Robert Ridge in 2004 while he was out hunting. They allowed me to keep this stone with me for several days so I could study it. I could see no obvious instrument marks in the crafting of the design on the stone, which fitted cosily in the palm of my hand. The fascinating thing about this stone is its unusual magnetic properties in the way that it spins the needle on a compass.

An exact replica of this design was created in a crop circle at Chisledon, Wiltshire, in the United Kingdom on the second of August 1996. Curiously, even natural grooves in the stone were replicated in this crop circle.

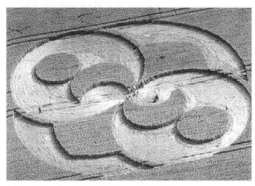 

Crop Circle Chisledon, Wiltshire, UK, 1996   Roswell Stone NM USA 2004

In my view, the matching designs in the Chisledon crop circle and the Roswell stone signify the life-giving solar, lunar, and galactic energies now being anchored on earth and, consequently, giving rise to the realisation of oneness consciousness within humanity.

THE REMARKABLE SOLSTICE OF JUNE 21, 2011

Many significant and memorable events brought about by certain cosmic configurations over the last three decades in particular, have contributed to stunning leaps in human consciousness. The Harmonic Convergence of August 16 and 17, 1987, the Harmonic Concordance of November 8 and 9, 2003, and the Cosmic Portal Transit of 11:11:11 are just three examples. Many have reported life-changing epiphanies during these potent times.

Speculation is rife as to what may occur on the solstice of December 21, 2012, when both the sun and the earth are in alignment with the galactic core, an event that only happens once every 26,000 years. Sadly, predictions of possibilities around this date are skewed to apocalyptic prophecies that engender debilitating fear. For some people these may prove to be self-fulfilling prophecies as some mayhem may indeed eventuate for those who focus upon and promulgate dark scenarios.

The good news is that these planetary and cosmic conditions throughout 2012 will awaken gradual enlightenment in many, which may peak on and around the December solstice, changing life as we know it on earth. No doubt, the following years up until 2020 will bring unimaginable and exciting changes to everyone who is sensitive to these energies and open to evolution. Imagine, just for example, the changes that would occur as a consequence of leaders in politics, business, and religious and spiritual organisations experiencing oneness with cosmic consciousness.

Prior to every change in the season, I spend a week or so embellishing my plans for the upcoming three months on how to enrich my life and the lives of others. The solstices and equinoxes that begin each new season are potent times, and a small miracle happened for me on the June solstice in 2011.

Many of my friends had been encouraging me to "do something" with my photos and I'd been contemplating how I could share a selection of them, along with some of my otherworldly experiences. I decided that the winter of 2011 would be a great time to put together a collection, so I took on a farm-sit while the owners travelled through Europe for two months. The isolated farmhouse bordered a densely forested national park and was in a virtual wilderness, as very few people ever ventured into the forest from that locale.

On the morning of the solstice, I had been contemplating the many things we can learn from trees. Some trees have become my muses, and I delight in getting to know certain ones on a personal basis. I contemplated my insights about how they support so much life; the produce they grow; their patience, ancient wisdom, and deep listening; and their silent connection to the divine.

On the afternoon of the solstice, I decided to explore a section of the forest I hadn't ventured into before. I gathered my trusty phone, which also acts as a camera, compass, and torch, and eagerly set off.

I headed into the pristine rainforest seen in these photographs and was very attentive as to where I was placing my boots and quietly mindful of any activity by nature spirits. As there were no paths, I allowed my intuition to lead the way while taking careful note of the new trail I was forging. After about two hours of exploring, I sat on a boulder to rest, drink in the sights, and listen to the symphony of bird sounds.

Just before dusk, I decided to return via some paddocks adjacent to the forest. As I was approaching the farmhouse, I discovered to my horror that my phone was gone. I searched every pocket again and again. What were the chances of finding my small black phone in the darkening, dense undergrowth or on the precarious rocky banks of the creek? I imagined they were slim at best.

I centred myself, quietly brought to mind the lessons I'd contemplated earlier in the day concerning trees, and determined to return to the forest to find my phone. I had only had it for two seasons, yet it was full of irreplaceable photos and information, so I carefully began retracing my steps.

Slowly and intuitively, I made my way back along my trail through the dense undergrowth. Whenever doubt surfaced, I simply refocused and impeccably followed my instincts again. I was quite calm, as a reassuring hand seemed to be guiding me. Who or what was that presence?

More than halfway back along my trail and nestled in long grass was my precious phone. I was filled with gratitude for my unseen friend and congratulated myself for listening so attentively as I happily returned to my writing cabin before darkness set in.

That night, I used the camera on my phone to take the remarkable series of photos that follows.

Spirit Orbs and Streams of Light

Solar and lunar energies anchor a massive influx of light and information to Mother Earth. All photos were taken in front of the same magnificent tree on the solstice of June 21, 2011.

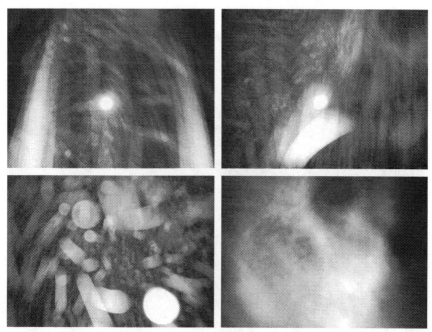

Anchoring massive influxes of Light, June Solstice 2011.

Pre-dawn the following morning.

CONSCIOUSNESS AND EXPERIENCE

The rainbow image shown on the back cover, in the full colour eBook, and below in grayscale illustrates my current view of how humans dwell within the dynamic frequencies of consciousness. The inner red circle encircling the meditating woman represents the third dimension of duality, time, form, and space. It is the world of opposites, physicality, limitation, and disconnection from Mother Father God.

We are so much more than red in the rainbow.

The additional rainbow colours signify "frontiers" or "borders," where form moves to formlessness and freedom and lack of awareness becomes full awareness and enlightenment. All the dimensions are interactive and merged in the same space or quantum field. They signify differing frequencies and states of consciousness that one may access instantly, or gradually, depending on his or her readiness, experiences, and choices.

Although there may be an infinite number of dimensions, discovery within these "seven" dimensions could take eternity. We learn, for example, that conditional love only exists in the third dimension, as do notions of polarity such as good and bad, right and wrong, in and out, and light and dark.

Multidimensional insights or intuitive flashes known as the quickening come from these many frequencies or dimensions of consciousness. Heightened consciousness states can be accessed by journeying out of body, meditation, stillness, chanting, trance, silence, intention, creativity, and in the dream state.

We are much more than red in the rainbow. As we consciously connect with the soul, we come to know what it knows. In our lifetime, many will evolve in consciousness and move from the third state of polarity consciousness to the fourth and fifth realms of spontaneous living, pure joy, and instant manifestation.

Dimensions are Merging

This photograph demonstrates doubles. In third dimensional reality, two friends and I had three goblets and one bowl containing our meal. My understanding is that there is a second identical world of the aluna or the faster vibrating etheric worlds, and my camera picked that up. Events occur in the aluna world before manifesting in the physical third dimension.

Mirror Worlds – a glimpse into another dimension.

Unity Consciousness

When it comes to unity, we could take our lead from the natural world, as seen, for example, by the synchronised behaviour of hundreds of starlings and large pods of dolphins. Mother Earth also supports myriad non-physical life forms such as spirit orbs that demonstrate unity consciousness as seen in their graceful, unified movement, similar to the birds and cetaceans.

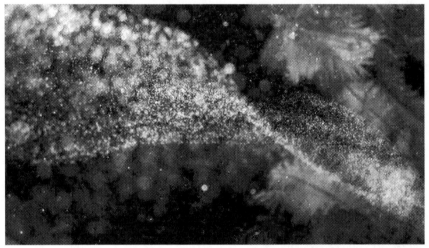

Unity – Spirit Orbs in flight.

Humanity is in the midst of a new renaissance, which in future history may be seen as a monumental spiritual renaissance. Sceptics and atheists are also experiencing the changes, and as a consequence some are altering their long-held perspectives about the nature of reality. Even as some scientists are bringing mysticism to their work, more business people are becoming philanthropic, some politicians more humanitarian, and some religious organisations more heart-centred.

Conscious thoughts, feelings, and choices are the training wheels for new multidimensional living. By 2020, I believe most humans will have had the insights, and perhaps even the personal experiences of pure consciousness, to make them aware that we live in the unified worlds of multidimensional existence.

The crystalline grid or consciousness scaffolding in and around the earth is enlivened and activated as our awareness evolves. The brain changes in structure as the pineal and other significant glands become reactivated, enabling easier and more open access to our many other selves. As the egoic, third-dimensional dualistic awareness rises into heart-centred love, it merges with the compassionate higher unlimited self, enabling greater consciousness both here on earth and in the celestial holy realms.

Changes brought about by the unification of the divine masculine and feminine attributes within are also impacting the birthing of the new human at this time. As the nature of our multidimensionality is being revealed, we become aware that we are also the creators and midwives to this new species.

All of us are, indeed, feeling and experiencing these changes, although some people are not yet ready to fully comprehend them. Symptoms such as sleeplessness, blurry vision, dizziness, and headaches can be painful and disconcerting. If you are suffering with the current transfiguration of your body and emotions, it is good to keep your eye on the prize. The newly awakened human will find heightened abilities for greater intuition, telepathy, empathy, clairvoyance, clairsentience, levitation, teleportation, instant manifestation, abundance, and even immortality and time travel.

THE NEW FRONTIER:
multidimensionality

Prior to visiting a foreign country, the discerning traveller studies the traditions of the people, the history, the geography, points of interest, and respectful protocols of that unfamiliar culture. I recommend similar research as we prepare to enter the domains of multidimensional places, parallel worlds, and new cultures. As part of this research, we might consider how we'll approach people and beings not of this earth.

I believe my photographs prove the existence of ephemeral life forms living in civilisations within, and beyond our third-dimensional reality. As the veils to other dimensions continue to thin, we realise the extent of the limitations within consensus reality that have been repeated exhaustively for eons of time.

Learning, loving, enjoyment, and spiritual evolution are surely the key purposes for life on this planet of immense diversity. We become aware of our 'other selves' when we risk venturing beyond our safe habits and the predictability of our comfort zones. As we delve deeper into the mysteries of our expansiveness we experience what it truly means to learn, to love, to enjoy, and to evolve spiritually.

Humanity is now at the momentous stage in its evolution where business as usual is obsolete, and we seek constructive change to the present largely dysfunctional fear-ridden reality. The luminous ones are co-creating life affirming and empowered lives by their positive intentions and conscious actions. The mystical gifts that have been there all along, yet hidden, become sublimely apparent as we venture to explore what lies within and beyond the new frontier.

THE LUMINOUS ONES
ARE UNVEILING THE
MYSTERIES OF
THE NEW FRONTIER

CEDAR RIVERS

Cedar Rivers taught in schools in Victoria for twenty-two years. In 1981, she established Spiral Booksellers, which she operated for fourteen years. This popular centre in Melbourne was a hub for spiritual networking and professional events. Her interests now include writing, spiritual counselling, photography, travel, and sustainable living. Cedar lives with her partner in rural New South Wales, Australia. Please visit her websites at www.cedar-rivers.com and www.thenewfrontiermultidimensionality.com